The Dealbreaker Diary

Red Flags, Reality Checks, & the Power of Walking Away

BY: KARIN BENT

Copyright © 2025 Karin Bent

All rights reserved.

ISBN: 979-8-218-87038-6

DEDICATION

To the woman I used to be —
the one who kept trying to understand what could never be explained.
The one who mistook chaos for passion, silence for peace, and inconsistency for "just how love is."
You survived every manipulation that tried to convince you that you were too much, too emotional, too sensitive, or too demanding.

You weren't. You were becoming. This one's for you, and every woman who finally realized that "walking away" isn't weakness. It's the beginning of coming home to yourself.

<u>Honorary Mention</u>

*And to **<u>HIM</u>**, the eight-year plot twist I never saw coming.*
*Thanks for all **your** drama, sneakiness, and explosive communication —*
*a chaotic trilogy that somehow added up to a masterclass in what love is **not**,*
and the very inspiration behind this book — which will hopefully
grace the coffee tables of many incredible people.

Amazing how one man's emotional coma can become another woman's awakening.
And to think… all those times you'd say, **"I'm not livin' that kind of life."**
You were right, you absolutely were not living a life where love or relationships mattered enough to make a legit consistent effort. Which is exactly why I finally walked out of it.

Some exits deserve applause —mine deserves a standing ovation.
Turns out the life you weren't willing to live is the one I'm finally thriving in.

"TOOTLES"

CONTENTS

AUTHOR'S NOTE   i

INTRODUCTION   iv

Chapter 1: Busy For Me, Free for TikTok   Pg 1

Chapter 2: All Sex, No Substance   Pg 7

Chapter 3: It's Your Fault I Hide It   Pg 11

Chapter 4: Don't Answer to You & I Coddle Noone   Pg 15

Chapter 5: Emotional Coma   Pg 21

INTERMISSION

Chapter 6: Drama, Drama, Drama   Pg 29

Chapter 7: Accountability Escape Artist   Pg 34

Chapter 8: Sorry, Not Sorry   Pg 39

Chapter 9: Someday, Maybe   Pg 44

Chapter 10: The Truth She Finally Knows   Pg 51

AUTHOR'S NOTE

I didn't exactly mean to write a book. I meant to reset from one relationship unlike any others I'd ever experienced. But when you spend eight years in a love story that occasionally feels like a fairy tale — and then suddenly flips into a psychological escape room every time you expect bare-minimum effort — well, I supposed you must put the plot somewhere. This is where mine landed.

There were days that felt magical. Beautiful, hilarious, connected, passionate. The kind of days that make your people roll their eyes and say, "Okay fine, maybe he's not that bad."

Then there were days when I would ask a very normal, very human question like, "Hey, what are we doing? "or "Can you please just be transparent with me?" and suddenly I was strapped into an emotional rollercoaster I didn't remember buying tickets for. Whiplash didn't even begin to cover it.

It's a special kind of hell to know, deep in your bones, that something is wrong — while simultaneously being told, in an infuriatingly calm tone, that you are the problem. That you are too sensitive. That you are expecting too much. That your intuition is "overreacting."

There's nothing quite like trying to repair a relationship while the other person is busy performing a disappearing act — emotionally, physically, spiritually — and you're stuck wondering if you're losing your mind or finally finding it. Here's the real kicker:

Walking away wasn't just heartbreaking — it was humiliating. Because when I left, there was no closure. **No moment of honesty. No softness.** Not even the dignity of sadness.

Just… indifference. Cold, sterile indifference — like someone unplugging a lamp.

One moment I was "the love of his life," and the next I was a UPS package he couldn't wait to return to sender — his idea of "amicability".

While I packed my life and tried not to crumble, he treated the end of eight years like a quick transaction, with no customer service, no refund, and no extended warranty. And, the extended family I'd made my own for so long followed suit, no questions asked.

The emotional wreckage? That was mine to deal with. Alone.

Meanwhile, I already knew exactly what would happen next — the instant moving on, the humble retelling of the breakup as though he were the noble hero who had ended it, when he didn't. The "I'm a private person. I don't share shit with anyone" ploy — where he waits for the right opportunity to toss out his usual, ***"She's a good girl, I loved her very much. We had some great times"***. Yet somehow, he still finds a way to slip in pieces of his delusional reality — the version where I'm painted as the "unstable" one. It's funny, in a tragic, ironic, dark-comedy sort of way. Because that's what this relationship was: a dizzying mix of euphoria, confusion, intensity, laughter, guilt, passion, invalidation, deep connection, deep disconnection, hope, disappointment, and the constant feeling that maybe — just maybe — I was asking for too much when all I really wanted were the basic elements of reciprocity.

I'm far from perfect—trust me, I have a whole highlight reel of questionable reactions. But that's the point: they were *reactions*. Responses to the chaos, mixed signals, and mental gymnastics he kept setting off in my head. This book isn't to shame him. And it isn't to make me the victim. It's to finally acknowledge the truth I lived through — with humor, clarity, hindsight, and a little bit of sass.

It's for anyone who stayed too long because the highs felt worth surviving the lows… until the lows became all that was left. It's for anyone who ever felt erased by someone they once loved. It's for anyone who needed closure and got silence instead.

Most of all, it's for the woman I was — and for every man or woman who has ever doubted their own reality in the presence of someone who never earned that power. If this book makes you laugh, cry, or whisper "holy crap, this is my life," then it's already doing its job.

Welcome to The Dealbreaker Diary.

INTRODUCTION

If you found this lying around and opened it — congratulations. You're now holding the bullshit decoder you didn't know you needed.

If you bought this book for yourself — hell yes. You're choosing peace, perspective, and personal power over the walking red flags you used to call "potential."

And if someone *gifted* it to you? Then someone in your life said, *"I love you… and you need this before you lose your mind."*

Whoever you are — accidental reader, intentional reader, or lovingly ambushed reader — you're here for a reason. Let's begin.

This isn't a romance novel, a journal full of gentle reflections, or a soothing TED Talk about empathy. This is the manual you wish someone had handed you the moment you thought a walking red flag was your soulmate.

Written by someone who has loved fiercely, lived deeply, and learned from every scar — and finally realized that some people define "effort" as a lifetime achievement award they earned the day they bought your favorite snack.

And here's the truth: If the relationship requires you to burn out, shut down, or sacrifice yourself and your world as you know it, just to keep the peace, that's not love — that's emotional demolition disguised as "just how I am."

So, this book? It's a collection of dealbreakers. Not theoretical ones. Not social-media buzzwords. Not the kind therapists gently unpack over six sessions. But the real ones — the patterns that drain you, confuse you, break you, and slowly disconnect you from the version of yourself you used to recognize.

The ones you don't fully understand until you've lived them. The ones you try to explain and justify until you're exhausted. The ones you forgive until you're empty.

If you're a woman reading this:

May you feel seen, validated, and just a little more powerful than you did before. Trust your instincts.

If you're a man reading this — whether by curiosity or conscience —Please keep your hands, ego, and defensiveness inside the vehicle at all times. This might sting, it might inspire you, or it might hit home for you with your own experience, depending on how honest you're willing to be with yourself.

Either way, growth looks good on everyone. So, grab a drink, take a breath, and prepare to be introduced to the face-slapping flags that taught me everything I needed to know about love, self-respect, and the power of walking away.

Let the dealbreakers begin.

CHAPTER 1
Busy for Me, Free for TikTok

CHAPTER 1

BUSY FOR ME, FREE FOR TIKTOK

If I'm doing all the initiating, carrying every conversation, and your best effort is a three-hour-late "hey" or a lazy emoji, we're just done. You're not mysterious; you're just under-invested.

We all have jobs, bills, families, workouts, chaos — and yet we all somehow find time to scroll, double-tap, or post nonsense. And most of us still find time to offer something to those we care about, in some form. That green dot next to your name doesn't lie my friend. This isn't about needing constant contact. It's about mutual initiative.

If I'm the only one driving the connection, especially in the beginning, then we don't have a connection — I'm not dating you… I'm managing you.

If you can't spare thirty seconds to start a conversation, send a respectful reply, or show actual interest, it's not because you're busy — it's because you're not prioritizing. And that same lack of initiative shows up everywhere else eventually. Consistency isn't clingy. Effort isn't demanding.

It's literally the ***bare minimum***. *If you can't start a conversation, don't start a relationship.*

NEWS FLASH — The "Too Busy" act isn't just digital — It's physical too.

People like this aren't just lazy communicators — they're lazy partners. Because the same human who can't send a text without breaking into a sweat is somehow even more exhausted at the idea of seeing you. Suddenly every attempt to make plans *(usually initiated by you)* becomes a logistical crisis for them —

"This week is crazy."

"Work wiped me out."

"I've got stuff I wanna do." (but they aren't sure what yet)

"We don't have to be attached at the hip."

"We'll see." *(translation: never unless you guilt me into it)*

Meanwhile? He has the energy to run errands, hit the gym, reorganize his garage, scroll TikTok for 3 solid hours, or take a spontaneous drive to nowhere — just not a drive to you.

And when he does show up?

It's only after you ask. Or hint. Or beg. Or do emotional calculus to phrase it in a way that won't "pressure" him. You end up managing his availability like you're scheduling a celebrity appearance: *"Hi, can you maybe tell me when you might plan to see me this week? No worries if not!"*

And he'll drop tiny hints that your gratitude is mandatory—like his very presence is a gift to be cherished. ***"See, I love you. I showed up like you asked me to"***. And sadly, you're probably so dazzled by his decision to show, that you can't help but hand-feed his ego with praise and appreciation — for bare minimum effort. Meanwhile, you're bending your work, your schedule, your life — while he's out there acting like hitting the highway toward you requires a passport and a medical clearance.

And the worst part? He'll insist he wants to see you — but mysteriously never plans anything. Because effort is free —but for him, it's apparently in short supply. Here's the truth nobody wants to admit:

If spending time with you was a priority, you wouldn't have to request it like PTO.

A person who's genuinely interested doesn't make you **ask** for his presence; he makes plans just as you do.

- **They show up.**
- **They drive.**
- **They initiate.**
- **They invest.**

They choose to be around you because it feels like home, not an obligation. A person who isn't interested? They'll let you carry all the effort, all the scheduling, all the energy, all the labor —and then call themselves "low maintenance" like it's a personality trait, not emotional negligence.

But here's the bottom line: Presence is effort. Effort is interest. If you must always nudge him to make an appearance, don't be fooled. He's not choosing you.

If I must always ask for your time, I don't want your time.

CHAPTER 2

All Sex, No Substance

CHAPTER 2

ALL SEX, NO SUBSTANCE

Let's address *that guy (and maybe girl)* — the one who thinks affection means grabbing, poking, squeezing, or cupping any body part that happens to be in arm's reach. Bruh…that's not intimacy. That's a toddler with hormones — *aka* manchild. To those guys…

If every time you walk past her you feel spiritually compelled to grope something, news flash — you're not being "passionate", you're just being grabby. Yes, we are thrilled that you're attracted enough to the package to want to inspect it; but please, calm your hands. There is a time and a place for affectionate touching and that doesn't always have to involve groping. Grabbing at me constantly doesn't make us closer. It makes me reconsider my escape routes. As for the sex…

I love sex — **great sex** — especially when there's chemistry that ignites something more than your zipper. But if your entire relationship skill set revolves around,

- *How fast can I get turned on?*
- *Where can I put it?*

- *Did I hit every spot?* or
- *Did I finish?*

I'm sorry to break it to you, but you're not partner-worthy material. You're just a horny Roomba. I'm not looking for romance novel foreplay, but **"let me hit that"** or **"wanna fuck?"** isn't exactly going to spark my fire.

The best way to claim victory for our ever-lasting, consistent pleasure in bed?

Start by trying to understand that for **most women**, genuine connection and sensuality equates to our ultimate climax, *not just bumping uglies*. And, unless I've explicitly told you otherwise, I'm not here to be your penis's plaything, or your grab-and-go entertainment.

Sex is incredible when it's built on trust, respect, and emotional intimacy. Otherwise, it's just synchronized sweating. If you think the real high comes from quantity over connection, go chase someone/something else with low-caliber sensuality to make *"your shit twitch"*. **Something inflatable, even**.

I'll wait for the person who understands that bedroom chemistry starts with energy, attention, effort, presence — **not** entitlement, not grabby hands, and not "this counts as intimacy, right?"

Because the sexiest thing someone can bring to the table isn't a perfect body or an Oscar worthy performance. It's emotional depth, intentional touch, and the ability to show up fully — clothed, unclothed, and everywhere in between.

If emotional depth ruins the mood for you, then sadly you've already hit your peak. So, I'll save mine for that mature someone whose intimacy bandwidth is measured in substance not seconds.

CHAPTER 3
It's Your Fault I Hide It

THE STUFF SHE COULDN'T UNHEAR...

"I'm not going round and round with you all day"

(because there was never any resolution)

CHAPTER 3

IT'S YOUR FAULT I HIDE IT

If your moral compass points to "it shouldn't bother you as long as I didn't physically do anything," congratulations — you've just earned a PhD in Selective Accountability.

You know the type: the ones who hide old flirty messages, answer DMs with a wink, or quietly delete a "hey stranger" text even if they didn't technically respond. They'll call that "respecting boundaries." *"I didn't want you to be hurt by that, so I got rid of it."*

Here's the thing — if you must hide it, clear it, or rename it in your phone, it's already a problem. Cheating isn't just a body thing; it's an integrity thing. Deleting proof doesn't make it harmless — it just makes it harder to catch. And continuing to hide things that your partner has already tried to address with you in a respectful, patient and tolerant way? Well, that's not forgetfulness. That's a deliberate decision. And decisions don't lie — people do.

And, when your intuition taps you on the shoulder and says, 'Look again' — because their own behavior trained you to? Oh, buckle up sweetie — suddenly **YOU** become the problem.

They'll twist it into:

"You shouldn't have looked."

"You invaded my privacy."

"Why go looking for trouble?"

"This I why I delete stuff, I don't want the drama." *(interpretation: I don't want to be held accountable in any way)*

As if your reaction to their deception is more offensive than the deception itself. It's Olympic-level blame-shifting: they light the match; you get blamed for noticing the fire. And please don't use the classic excuse: *"I didn't want to have to deal with this all over again."*

No, you didn't want to have to answer for it — the first time around . There's a difference. If you truly care about someone, you don't risk their trust or plant doubts, questions, or insecurities by playing games that require hiding, deleting, or disguising anything. Nothing good in a relationship comes from secrecy — especially the kind you've pre-edited before anyone can see.

Oh, and that infamous guilt-trip: *"Hey, well if you can't just trust me when I say I'm not doing anything, I guess we have problem."* Yes, we do have a problem. And it's not me. If you think "not replying" counts as emotional neutrality… reality check: you're not protecting me from feelings—you're protecting yourself from responsibility.

Grown adults in healthy relationships don't operate in gray zones of technicalities. They operate in transparency. Because if you care about someone, you don't risk their trust for the cheap thrill of feeling "wanted" by someone else — even if you never touch them. Nor do you hide stuff to prevent having to answer for it.

If you have to hide it to 'avoid drama,' you're not being considerate —

you're just being selfishly calculated.

CHAPTER 4

I Don't Answer to You & I Coddle No One

CHAPTER 4

I DON'T ANSWER TO YOU & I CODDLE NOONE

Ah yes — the empathy deficient, selective giver/helper.

The one who does plenty of household upkeep — *of their choosing, of course* — and secretly believes they deserve sainthood for it. The kind who subtly acts like whatever they do is automatically far superior to anything you may do— and they're not shy about letting you know it with that special passive-aggressive banter of theirs. They'll drop insulting little gems like:

"I guess we should just hire a maid."

As if you're sunbathing in a lawn chair watching them struggle — which is ironic, because they'll pull that exact move on you the second **you** ask for help with something they don't want to deal with. And just when you think everything's fine, they'll randomly explode on you with some delusional rant about everything you "don't do" (according to them):

"You need to step it up," *or* ***"I can't do everything around here,"*** as if you haven't been silently carrying the emotional, mental, and physical load that keeps the entire relationship functioning.

And then there's the other flavor — the "quality-control specialist."

The one who helps just enough to claim credit, then turns around and critiques how you do your part. The partner who nitpicks, belittles, and measures every contribution like it's a competition. They'll secretly (or not so secretly) micromanage everything you do and conveniently ignore ALL the other things you handle daily. All the unseen labor — the stuff you handle instinctively just to keep life livable — and the things you willingly volunteer for on their behalf because you're invested… unlike them.

You know the type: the person who can handle their half of the chores but goes conveniently blind the second something specifically matters to you.

You're gleefully knee-deep in holiday decorating, reorganizing a room, prepping for a family party, or tackling a home project that means something — and they're planted on the couch saying:

"That's all you babe. I don't have to be involved in everything you do." or *"Don't expect me to sacrifice my time just because you decided to overwhelm yourself."*

They don't **offer** to help with what you're doing. They may do so, but only when you explicitly ask — and even then, it's with the energy of someone being handed a prison sentence. They'll sigh, drag their feet, complain, or act like you're asking for the moon instead of basic support. Or they'll selectively assist with whatever *they* deem important. Or worse, they will mock and minimize whatever it is you're doing — dropping comments like:

"What are you talking about, I did all the real work. All you ever do is meal prep and make things look pretty."

And the encore?

They'll add to your confusion by selectively "giving you credit" for certain jobs well done; but this is the same person who will then hit you with a behind-closed-doors, top-volume tirade about how your efforts barely graze the bottom of their inflated expectations.

Willingly offering to help to decorate, prep for a party, clean before/after company or do things that weren't on **your to-do list** doesn't make you a martyr —it makes you supportive. If you think *"I did the windows and power washed, my job's done and far outweighs your contributions,"* you've missed the assignment entirely.

Here's the thing — it's not about who's capable. It's about consideration. Partnership isn't limited to chores; it's showing up for each other in ways that matter, even when it's not your personal passion project and even when it's inconvenient. For instance —

How about when you're sick and needing a little extra care and compassion?

Well, this is the same micro-managing housemate who will declare *"I don't coddle anyone!"* So, if they're not flat-out ignoring or avoiding you (until they need something), you'll get a performance evaluation instead of comfort — the kind packed with vague 'you should really…' advice from someone who won't do a damn thing unless prompted like a malfunctioning Alexa. Or worse, they will literally mock you for asking for that much needed hug, snuggle or gentleness. They'll sarcastically trot over to you, with utter annoyance, pat you on the head, and speak to you like a child while saying *"Awwwww what, you're sick? you need a hug?"*

The type that, if you're discomfort is inconveniencing their routine, won't hesitate to toss out remarks like:

"If you can't settle yourself the fuck down and go to sleep, you should just go home/go elsewhere." (translation: my own comfort is far more important than your discomfort)

If you're with someone who always treats effort and showing up for you like a massive burden, sorry friend — you've found yourself someone exceptional. Exceptional under their terms, within their comfort zone, and only when nothing is required of them that wasn't on their internal checklist.

Real relationships are **NOT** built on:

"I'll help when it's convenient for me," or **"I'll show care and compassion only when it absolutely necessary."**

Real relationships are built on showing up — consistently, willingly, and without treating your needs as irritations or your efforts as inferior.

If you only 'help' to control the outcome or avoid discomfort — you're not a partner, you're a shitty project manager with a connection deficit

CHAPTER 5
Emotional Coma

CHAPTER 5

EMOTIONAL COMA

There's a special kind of partner who swears they "don't do all that emotional stuff," as if empathy were an optional upgrade package, that isn't part of the deal they negotiated.

Cry?

You'll get a blank stare; or worse, laughed at.

Get upset about something they did or didn't do *(but should've)*?

You're "overreacting."

Need reassurance, comfort, or a deeper conversation? Suddenly it's:

"Come on, I don't wanna talk about serious stuff," or ***"I shouldn't have to reassure you,"*** *(from the same person caught repeatedly hiding texts, lying to you or dismissing you)* OR ***"I'm not doing this right now."***

But the real kicker?

When things get genuinely emotional — when you're hurt, shaken, or in distress because of ***their*** behavior — their emotional coma becomes a full-blown rage-filled disappearing act.

They'll leave the room mid-conversation, pretend not to see your calls, or tuck themselves into bed while you're still standing in the ruins of a conflict that never needed to exist. But ask for emotion, accountability, or a peaceful landing? You'll get hit with ridicule, rage, or character assassination so unexpected it knocks you into a whole new level of disbelief. They'll do nothing — absolutely nothing — to settle the tone, offer peace, or even acknowledge your pain… even when you're begging for it.

Because in their world, disappearing isn't abandonment — it's ***"the only way to stop the drama."*** Drama that ***they*** often created, escalated, and then conveniently blamed on you. They can watch you cry, crumble, or shut down emotionally, and instead of stepping up, they step out.

- **No comfort.**
- **No accountability.**
- **No reflection.**
- **Just escape.**

And the next day, they'll act like you're the one who "took things too far," rewriting the entire event so they can sleep at night, and you can question your own sanity. They'll expect you to ***"move on"*** and ***"let it go"*** like nothing had ever happened at all. They'll keep you just secure enough by not dumping you *this* time, but trust —they're already logging every detail they'll later spin into your 'bullshit drama' as the sole cause of all those ***"all-night, drag-out fights"*** they've vowed never to have again.

The real dealbreaker is this:

If your heartbreak barely registers with them, if your feelings are always "too much," and if emotional intimacy is treated like an inconvenience, you're not dealing with someone who lacks skills — you're dealing with someone who lacks genuine *"give a fuck"* paired with the emotional intelligence of a wet noodle.

Because someone who cares doesn't disappear at the exact moment you need them most. Someone who cares can pause their anger long enough to show compassion and work toward mutual resolution—because peace with you matters more than their comfort or ego.

If you can ignore my heartbreak and call it "avoiding drama," then avoiding you is the best self-care I'll ever practice.

INTERMISSION

If you've made it this far without throwing your phone, crying, or texting your therapist—you're already doing better than most of us did mid-trauma bond.

This is your moment to pause…

sip something caffeinated or spiked…

and mentally review all the red flags you absolutely ignored because:

- 🚩 he "had potential,"
- 🚩 he "went through a lot,"
- 🚩 he "wasn't like this in the beginning,"
- 🚩 he "swore he'd change,"

or the classic:

"But when it's good, it's so good." Uh-huh.

So is chocolate lava cake.

Doesn't mean it should be your entire diet. This intermission exists so you can:

Laugh,

Cringe,

Self-reflect,

Feel validated,

and maybe whisper "holy shit, this is my life" to yourself.

Consider this page your emotional palate cleanser.

Take a breath.

Stretch.

Hydrate.

Reassure your future self that you will never again date a man-child whose emotional growth was last updated sometime around IOS 4. And when you're ready?

Flip the page.

Because we're only getting stronger, funnier, and more self-aware from here.

CHAPTER 6
Drama Drama Drama

"I'm not doing this if anyone can hear."

CHAPTER 6

DRAMA, DRAMA, DRAMA

Some people talk. Some people communicate.

And then there's him — the man who treats a simple talk like you're dragging him into a trial, a hostage standoff, or a made-for-TV meltdown. With this type, even the softest, gentlest, most carefully *pre-scheduled* or worded "hey, can we talk about something?" turns instantly into:

The silent sigh, the nervous pacing, eye's elsewhere, or the patent-pending, pretend-I'm-listening head nods and repeated "okays."

Anything emotionally meaningful that you are wishing to discuss — literally anything — becomes unnecessary "drama," even if he doesn't show it immediately or distinctively.

You calmly express a concern? *"Here we go again."*

You bring up something hurtful or unresolved? (because there is no resolution w/this person and usually repeat violations) Then it's *"You need to let this go." "How long am I gonna have to hear about this?"* or *"are you gonna punish me forever?"*

If you push for clarity in conversations filled with deflection, blame shifts and dismissals? *"Enough is enough — just stop yourself! If you can't stop yourself, then we're done!"*

You look for reassurances? *"I'm not having a serious conversation right now."*

You try to finish the conversation? *"When I say I'm done, I'm done. You should know when to leave me the fuck alone."*

And watch out — the moment you recognize how unfair and twisted it all is, the second you push back against the fake listening, the needless anxiety, the defensiveness, or the shouting, name-calling, and threats… suddenly *you* become the problem. The aggressor. The "one who can't ever let things go." Because real acknowledgment and accountability? **Please**. That's his kryptonite — watch him disintegrate and disappear on contact. But it doesn't stop there.

He won't want to discuss anything if:

- someone is in the same house
- a window is open
- a neighbor might hear
- you're in public

If he senses even a 1% chance someone could witness how the conversation will likely escalate, he will literally scan the room, check the surroundings, shut doors, lower his voice, or refuse to talk altogether because deep down he knows the way he communicates isn't normal. However, in his delusional reality, he absolutely believes it is YOU who will create the chaos and therefore the need to mute the conversation before it even starts.

The truth?

Deep down, he knows it would expose him — and the chaotic, wildly unnecessary reactions he keeps trying to pass off as normal. If he can't control the narrative, he won't have the conversation. This is the man who escalates fast:

Deflection → denial → blame-shifting → anger → explosive backlash → silence → exits → abandonments → and the grand finale: discard.

Nearly, every — single — time. And somehow you become the villain *he* needs saving from.

That "nearly" part? That's the real mind twister. Because he's not *always* dismissive or explosive — just enough to make you question your own delivery, your sanity, and whether the conversation even needed to exist in the first place. You're left hurt, confused, and desperate for resolution… while he walks away, shuts down emotionally, or threatens to end the relationship because he can't handle a normal adult discussion.

This isn't miscommunication. This is communication sabotage. Real partners don't weaponize the idea of "drama" to avoid accountability or compromise. They don't punish you for being human or having normal reactions. They don't make every difficult moment your fault.

Normal partners want resolution — not escape routes.

If "we need to talk" sends you into fight-or-flight, stay single — that's the only relationship you're equipped for.

CHAPTER 7
Accountability Escape Artist

CHAPTER 7

ACCOUNTABILITY ESCAPE ARTIST

Some people take responsibility. Some people apologize.

And then there's him — the man who treats accountability like it's radioactive. No matter what happens, no matter what he does, no matter how clear the evidence is, one thing is guaranteed:

It will never **really** be his fault.

Ever.

You bring up something hurtful? He'll trivialize it.

You raise a concern? He'll dodge it.

You show him the pattern? He'll deny it. Or blame you for it.

You quote something he literally just said? He'll rewrite it.

This is the man who can watch you drown in the aftermath of his behavior and still point to the water and say: "See what you caused?" in his own subtle manipulative way.

He'll redirect, minimize, distract, or resurrect something you might've done six months ago just to avoid sitting with the discomfort of his own actions. He'll dig up *your* worst moments (*reactions*) like an emotional archaeologist just to avoid talking about his own mess.

Try to talk calmly?

You're "making a big deal out of nothing."

Try to clarify?

You're "twisting my words."

Try to hold him accountable?

You're hit with: ***"always with this bullshit drama, drama, drama."***

And watch out! Bring up anything while mildly buzzed and he'll declare you an unhinged, "nasty" alcoholic — not because it's true, but because it's easier than owning his shit.

And just when you think he might get it — when he pulls out the dramatic sigh and the solemn face — he hits you with the infamous:

"Fine. I take full responsibility. For everything"

Except... he can't tell you what he's supposedly taking responsibility for. Because he's not actually owning anything — he's just throwing out the Magic Words™ to shut you up and end the conversation.

- ⚑ **No reflection.**
- ⚑ **No understanding.**
- ⚑ **No change.**

Just a verbal band aid slapped over a bullet hole. He has a million tricks:

Emotional smoke bombs→ *Topic changes*→ *Selective memory* → *Fake confusion* → *Pretend victimhood*

- *"That never happened"*
- *"You're remembering it wrong"*
- *"I'm not doing this all day."*
- *"I'm not goin' round and round with you."*

By the time he's done, you'll question your feelings, your memory, and your sanity — because the Accountability Escape Artist's greatest talent is making you feel guilty for having a perfectly normal emotional response to his behavior.

He doesn't resolve conflict; **he evades it.**

He doesn't repair harm; **he repackages it.**

He doesn't reflect inward; **he redirects outward — straight onto you.**

Because the truth is simple: He cannot tolerate seeing himself as the cause of anything uncomfortable — doing so would be a hit to the well-hidden, but iconically delusional perception he (*secretly*) has of himself. So instead, he will offer you breadcrumbs disguised as understanding as he sells you the story that *you* are the cause of everything.

And the longer you stay, the easier that lie is to believe. Make no mistake — a partner who refuses to offer real acknowledgement or take accountability is not protecting his peace — he's protecting his ego.

And there's no relationship on earth strong enough to survive one person doing all the emotional heavy lifting while the other sits comfortably in denial.

If you can't own your actions, then you don't deserve access to mine — especially the ones that keep this relationship alive.

CHAPTER 8
Sorry... Not Sorry

CHAPTER 8

SORRY, NOT SORRY

Some people apologize because they mean it. Some people apologize because they truly want to heal something.

And then there's him — the man whose apologies are nothing more than conversational duct tape: flimsy, temporary, and guaranteed to fall off the second things get uncomfortable again. This is the Professional Apologizer — the one who says "sorry" with the same enthusiasm most people use to close pop-up ads.

Fast.

Automatic.

Thoughtless.

And completely disconnected from any actual accountability. He'll dish out apologies like:

"I'm sorry you feel that way." (not an apology — a dodge)

"Fine, I said I'm sorry!" (not remorse — annoyance)

"I already apologized, what more do you want?" (not understanding — pressure to drop it)

"I'm sorry for everything." (the all-purpose apology used when he has no idea what he's apologizing for — and no intention of finding out)

"I take full responsibility." (not clarity — a performance)

And the all-time classic:

"Can we just move on?" (translation: please stop reminding me of what I did because I have zero intention of changing it)

His apologies aren't for healing. They're for convenience. They're for ending the conversation, not correcting the behavior.

He doesn't apologize to make things better — he apologizes to make you be quiet.

- **No reflection.**
- **No depth.**
- **No acknowledgement.**
- **No discomfort.**

Just a quick verbal offering to reset the clock on the same behavior he will likely repeat again next week — and you know it. Because with him, the cycle is always predictable:

Hurt → "sorry" → repeat → deny → "sorry" → repeat → escalate → "sorry" → start over.

His apologies aren't doorways — they're revolving doors, and you're the one getting dizzy. And if you bring up the same issue again later (because of course it comes back)?

Once again, *you're* the problem:

"I'm not doing this again with you."

"I said sorry a hundred times."

"Why can't you just let things go?" or *"Why do you have to go on and on and on?"*

See the theme here? Here's the truth:

The reality is that he doesn't really believe he has anything to apologize for in the first place! Because to him, whatever it is = "bullshit drama". Therefore, he wants forgiveness without growth. Reconciliation without accountability. Peace without real effort. Comfort without change. He wants the benefits of apology without the responsibility of transformation.

But an apology without action is **NOT**, and never will be, an apology. It's a performance. A rehearsed script. A tactic. A manipulative reset button.

And you deserve someone who repairs — not someone who repeats.

Your "sorry" isn't accountability — it's the snooze button on the same bullshit. And honey, I'm wide awake now.

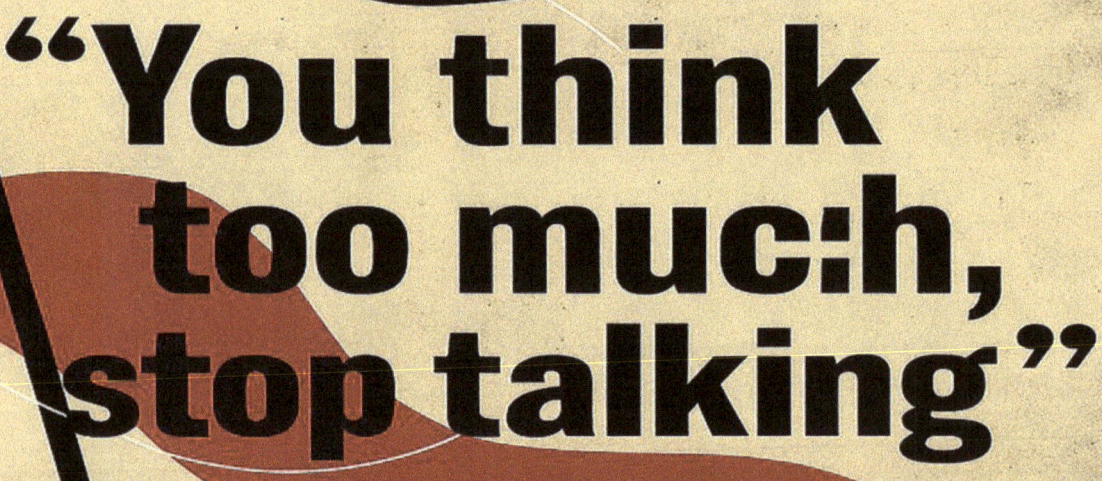

THE STUFF SHE COULDN'T UNHEAR...

"You think too much, stop talking"

(whenever she'd try to talk about *ANYTHING* that mattered to her)

CHAPTER 9

SOMEDAY, MAYBE

Or is it "Maybe someday". Does it really matter?

There's a certain kind of partner who will swear up and down that they're "committed," with all those endearing little nuggets like: *"I'm in it to win it," "you're the only one," "you're a keeper,"* and *"you're my forever"* …

as long as the future stays at a safe, theoretical distance where nothing requires action. This is the Future Faker — the man who will confuse you enough to entertain every next-step conversation *you* initiate, but never, ever start one himself.

Not once.

Not ever.

Not even by accident.

Want to talk about living together? Sure — someday.

Buying a house? Maybe — eventually *(as long the where is most convenient for me)*.

Marriage? Yeah — maybe someday, when the time is right (*but don't ask me when that is*).

A weekend getaway that requires choosing a date? "Possibly" (*if you let me ultimately micromanage the when, where and how*).

He'll sit there and engage with you in these conversations, nodding like he's on board, contributing just enough to keep you hopeful — but his answers are always subtly wrapped in:

"We'll see." I mean… I'm not against it."

"Could be cool someday."

"I'm open to the idea."

"I'm not going anywhere; we don't need everything planned out"

"Maybe someday."

Spoiler:

All those "maybe somedays" **never** actually get planned out – **not by him anyway**.

Because he has no actual intention of moving anything forward — he just doesn't want to lose you while standing still. Because that would make him look bad.

And then there's the ultimate illusion of commitment — the line he falls back on anytime you express wanting more clarity, more plans, or more direction:

"I'm here with you, aren't I? I'm not goin' anywhere. Isn't that enough?"

As if his physical presence — inconsistent, conditional, and often emotionally unavailable — should magically substitute for actual lifetime commitment. OR

"You know I'm not a planner. I fly by the seat of my pants. If you don't like that…."

It's the same man who can look you straight in the face during an argument and say something like:

"I'm done with you; we are done! I'm not livin' this kind of life!"

The same man who has literally threatened to leave you on the side of the road, or at a hotel just to "end" a conflict that didn't even need to be a conflict—and then act like it's your fault, leaving you scrambling to manage the emotional fallout….and then expect you to erase that from your heart like it never happened. And sadly, you try, and try, and try again. Because you're so trauma bonded by this point, you don't know how to let go, never mind try to process that level of rejection.

But in his world, threatening the relationship counts as normal behavior — but you asking for real commitment that involves actions that match words? **Whoa, relax… that's 'a lot.'** You ask for reassurance, and he acts like you're after one of his organs, but his dramatic breakup threats? Oh, that's just him 'keeping it real'.

And if any progress does happen? It's never because *he* led the way. It's because YOU dragged the entire relationship forward like a one-woman moving company. You planned it.

You pushed the conversation.

You followed up.

You reminded him.

You initiated again.

You brought it up gently.

You brought it up firmly.

You brought it up even after all the bullshit because you 100% invested in growth with him.

And when you do finally call out his lack of initiative toward growth? Suddenly he's got a thousand excuses, each one seasoned with just enough passive-aggressive blame to imply *you* — and your so-called ***"bullshit drama"*** — are the real reason he won't make such big plans.

Sometimes the only reason anything happens at all is because the pushing turned into frustration, the frustration turned into a fight, and the fight forced him to throw you a breadcrumb just to keep the peace and the illusion of life-long genuine commitment.

And that brings us to the masterpiece of Future Faking: The Fake Engagement — aka the ***"maybe someday"*** ring that was never a legit engagement.

You've got the ring. You had the moment. People congratulated you. It looked like the commitment you'd asked for. It felt like a commitment. You even felt happy, relieved and hopeful that you wouldn't have to forever remain the "girlfriend" until age 75.

Except… it wasn't that type of commitment at all. And deep down, you knew it.

Because he never actually said the words. Never followed through on the meaning, despite your pleas for him to do so years later. Never had a plan. Never treated it like a real step toward anything different at all.

It was a symbolic pacifier — A shiny gesture meant to buy time, quiet questions, and delay the next conversation about actual growth together. And later?

He'll say things like:

"You took it the wrong way."

"It wasn't supposed to mean all that."

Right — because nothing with him ever "means all that."

Not plans.

Not promises.

Not milestones.

Not the ring.

Not the effort required to grow a real future.

And the worst part? Once you finally push for clarity — months or years following that so called "engagement" — you'll get the gut punch of an encore — said with delusional arrogance and even with that painfully devious giggle: **"Well, look you. And all the bullshit drama, drama, drama. And you think I wanna marry you"** (Translation: *You're the instability, not them.*) And that "maybe someday" promise suddenly morphs into, **"I'm not sure I ever want to get married again"** — a statement never once uttered by him in all the attempted conversations had over 8 long years.

Enough to jolt you straight into reality, complete with the bonus package of confusion, anger, hurt, and heartbreak.

The truth?

With him, the future is always out there somewhere — vague, blurry, selfishly one-sided, and conveniently unreachable. Just enough to keep you hoping. Never enough to keep you progressing.

If your timeline is built entirely on "someday maybe," I'm going to assume that's also where you filed me — and baby, I don't live in the "pending" folder.

CHAPTER 10
The Truth I Finally Know